# WILD SWIMMING

JOHN RIORDAN

# Wild Swimming

DROMBEG BOOKS

ISBN: 978-1-9993529-1-2

Prepared for publication by

DROMBEG BOOKS
*Leap, Skibbereen, County Cork, Ireland*





*Biographical note*
John Riordan and his wife Gill moved from Dublin to
West Cork in 2008 to avail of a place for his daughter
Laurie in CoAction Skibbereen, where she attends the
Day Centre. He was educated by the Christian Brothers
in O'Connell's School, North Richmond Street, Dublin,
and University College Dublin. His work has been
published in *Brain of Forgetting,* an on-line international
literary magazine. *Wild Swimming* is his third poetry
collection, following  *After the Storm* (2017) and  *Into the
Wind* (2018). John  is a member of the Clonakilty Writers'
Group, which meets in the town's public library every
second Thursday at 11am throughout the year.

# Acknowledgements

Thank you, first of all, to my walking companions, John Mac Mahon, Laurie Riordan, Maggie, Alan O'Dwyer, and Carmel Somers, and to my family, friends, relations and neighbours in Reenogrena and County Cork who put up with my eccentricities; to Nick Smith and all the members of the Clonakilty Writers' Group, including Moze, Sebastian, Claire, Michael, Lorenza, Colette, Ann Dineen, Mary Rose, Afric, and Sean (RIP); to Nick and Kathy Weber; to my siblings Richard, Patrick, William Michael and Maggie and to Gill, my wife, constant companion and mentor; finally to Maurice Sweeney for his help in preparing this book for publication and making it such an enjoyable experience.

# Contents

*You ask whether your verses are good. You have asked others before. You are looking outward, and that, above all, you should not do now.*

*Nobody can counsel and help you, nobody. There is only one single way.*

*Go into yourself. Search for the reason that bids you to write; find out if it is spreading its roots in the deepest places of your heart. Acknowledge to yourself whether you would have to die if it were denied you to write. This above all—Ask yourself in the stillest hour of night: must I write? If you meet this earnest question with a strong and simple "I must", then build your life according to this necessity. Your life, even in its most indifferent and slightest hour must be a sign of this urge and a testimony to it.*

RAINER MARIA RILKE
(*Letters to a Young Poet*)

# Winter walk

We walked for a day in Wicklow
on the white wasteland of ice
over the lake at Ballyknockan
seeing four different solitary foxes
on winter walkabout, seeking a mate.
You spied a flock of fifty long-tailed tits
twittering and whispering
against the cold,
sheltering in the hawthorn hedges
along the lake shore,
gaining sanctuary.

# Harvey

A thunder clap signals Harvey's arrival
at our camp near Inlet in the Adirondaks.
Silver rods of heavy rain
herald a severe thunderstorm,
moving black barbecues
around like Daleks.
The flag flaps harder,
stars and stripes blur,
trees bend,
lake water foams round the jetty,
garden ornaments topple,
picnic tables and chairs take to the air.
On television, programme interruptions
scream tornado warnings,
but not for our part
of upstate New York.
Forty miles an hour winds
keep us comfortably indoors,
in awe of this weather,
mild for our time in this place.

# Dark Side

What sensual pleasures lie
on the dark side of the moon?

Love under tables, in the back of cars,
in tiny cubicles after nights in bars?

Holding tight
in empty hotel rooms
wherever people meet.

Eyes signal "yes".
A gesture, a sigh,
and afterwards,
what to do when passions die?

# Bushy Park

*May 2006*

A hungry fox
got the cob.
Weeks later
five curious cygnets
floated off the island
mother in tow.

How did she manage on her own
to feed and protect them?
Like Peggy did
when a coronary
wrung the neck
of Bill's too young heart,
leaving six of us to thrive.

# Autumn in Reenogrena

A hollow wind blows over the high ditch
as a flock of rooks rise together
from the yellow-cropped ground,
their foraging disturbed.
Christy's Big Field dips over the hill,
holding freshly packed bales of silage and streams of
    hay,
the ground-work done until the giant
tractors turn the soil again.
A wily grey crow takes off from its perch on the
    telephone pole
while two black, red-beaked choughs continue to
    squabble like lovers,
ignoring me as I pass under their hangout opposite the
    green barn.
The land releases a sigh after the year's work,
a great year for growth.

I feel the earth's core pulsating beneath me.

# Ar scáth a chéile

*Eileen Hurley*

Walk the roads round Kilfinnan, Reenogreena, Carrigluskey, Maulmoreen and Cregg on a good day and you will surely meet Eileen Hurley out enjoying the sunshine and be greeted with an enquiry about your family. Or it could be concerned news about a neighbour or the success of fund-raising for local charities. She lives near Richard's Cross beside her late brother Billy's house where her sister-in-law Breege lives.

Eileen's brother Pat lives and farms down the road in their original family homestead in Reenogreena. Eileen was born in 1941 and Pat in 1938. They both went to Reenogrena National School. "The national school was naturally at the heart of the area, being a school but also because people came there to cast their votes at election time," recalls Eileen. "It was a tough school where everyone learned their sums. Our house had plenty of books about the place so we had it easier with other subjects.

"In those days we drew water from wells. There was no piped water. Unlike now, there was no shortage of local grocery shops: in Kilfinnan, the Creamery, Paddy Mahoney's and Fortune's in Glandore, a shop in Hayes's Bar and a post office and bakery in the village. Wolfes

had a shop on the Black Hill. Now you can't get a
bottle of milk or a loaf of bread locally at the weekend.
There was a big market for Glandore-grown violets
on the London Flower Market sold through an agent
there.
"I preferred the simple life then. If you didn't have the
money, you did without."

She studied science with the Sisters of Charity in
Dunmanway—"They were the nuns with wings"—and
received a certificate. She did clerical work in London
for Westminster City Council. "I believed that Irish
emigrants who worked outdoors were the happiest,
perhaps because of our closeness to the land." Eileen
also worked with Christina Goulandris in Shorecliff, a
house she shared with her husband, Tony O'Reilly.

Eileen is not ashamed to be called a religious person
with a strong faith in God. "You have nothing if you
don't have that. We all need a spiritual connection
and a sense of the importance of community support.
Isolation and the lack of human contact can kill a
community. *Ar scáth a chéile a mhairimid.* We used to
have a great drama group here run by one of the priests.
There was dancing in Crowley's hall in Union Hall
and Hodnett's in Rosscarbery. Not to mention pattern
dancing in Trá an Aonaigh once upon a time, which I
remember my aunt Sissy talking about.

Eileen believes deeply in the Christian message of "love
thy neighbour". She enjoys her fine day rambles with
the sole assistance of a walking stick. "Your health is
your wealth."

# For M

We talked,
the three of us
on the night
you arrived
at our door.
Not sure if you
were going or staying,
you sat,
and your stillness
held us there,
sharing the beauty
of a long moment.

# Dodder

Brown Dodder water flowed deep,
rippled white over stones,
tumbled and curled in rapid waves.
Rain dripped on me from leaves of oak chesnut, elm
    and lime,
fishbones etched on beech leaves.
A yellow wagtail flickered through low branches.
A solitary heron on the green football pitch
stooped to pick worms from the grass,
was disturbed, rose. and landed further on,
content to enjoy the wet, wriggling bounty
of easy pickings.

# DNR

I keep waking up
with this thing going round in my head.
If you find me lying on the narrow road
where I walk every morning,
my faithful hound licking my face,
tell the ambulance driver
I don't want to be resuscitated. .

If I survive an explosion in my head
or a clot blocks my heart,
this is my will:
please, let me go.
Beloved, children and grandchildren, dear friends,
please remember me as I was.
living a lucky life,
going quietly in the end.

# Drama on Warren Strand

The Warren dog walkers are out in force:
John Mac, known by all, meets Mickey Brien,
nature lover and fellow dog-walker
who tells him about a stranded seal on Warren Strand,
abandoned by the tide, helpless and vulnerable.
"Leave the animal alone. The mother will be back on
    the incoming tide," is the official advice,
confirmed by Siobhan from Cobh, walking the beach,
talking on her mobile to the Seal Sanctuary in Kerry .
Pat the Wren calls John,worried about gathering canine
    interest in the seal's predicament.
The seal lovers decide to act.
Six rescuers gather round,
including two young women in wet suits
who have spotted the seal mother's head
bobbing in the incoming waves.
The rescue party begins to help the seal,
slowly easing it inch by inch,
gently lifting it towards deeper water.
Sensing buoyancy, the seal takes over
and begins its swim to freedom and motherly care.
The newly formed Warren Seal Rescue Group votes to
    adjourn
for a celebratory drink in Nolan's in Rosscarbery.
Job done. No bother!
"Just like Mac," quips James to his wife, "making a fuss
    over a stranded seal."
"The seal was haunted "says John.

# Hungry Hill

We leaned into the cold north westerly,
climbing till the path disappeared,
then clambered over rocks to look down
at the wind ploughing
 furrows on the surface of the mountain lake.
You were reminded of Machu Pichu, you said,
layers of stone lying there
since some ancient upheaval.
We walked and scrambled down the hill,
testing ourselves on little alpine rocky descents.
Cold sweat on my back,
I froze like a fridge magnet
half way down a sheer face,
and you talked me down by another route.
We mined deep into our lives and,
trailing our memories,
rested on a crag,
eating Kathy's gourmet sandwiches,
olives and sausages from pigs fattened on Durrus
    cheese.
Seeking water to sustain us,
we descended through the soaked land
and threw our naked bodies
into the lake,
the cold shocking our spirits
into a calm awareness.

# Dogma

A scared eleven-year-old boy
wondered about the teaching.
His body shaking with fear,
he stood up from the bench
and asked, "Please, sir,
how can we be members
of the one true Church?
What about the millions
of Chinese and  African people?"
The Christian Brother scowled
and walked silently round the classroom.
"Shut up, Riordan," he said.
"You will read your way
out of the Church before long."

# Wakening

*Summer 2018*

From my bed in the valley
I see how the hill wears a coat of grey mist,
soon to burn to blue sky
patch-worked with
cotton clouds.
I hear the excitement
of waking blackbirds,
the lonely *kee-kee*
of young peregrines
flying high over me.
The cold sea promises
a shocking immersion,
supercharging my circulation,
clearing my head
till I am truly awake!

# Sacrament

Her feet slipped from her sandals,
to walk bare on a well-trodden winter wet grass path.
She held my hand as we walked
to a sleeping mountain ash,
where she gripped the v-shaped branches,
pressing and pulling herself in and out,
till her body began to tire.

"Let's do another round of the fields," she said,
 drawing fresh energy from the earth.

# Smudge

The front door was slightly ajar.
I heard a deep guttural noise
when Smudge our cat
brushed in triumphantly,
holding a live mouse
in her mouth.
She dropped and scooped
the doomed animal playfully
backward and forward.
I picked her up with her prey
and placed them outside
to let nature take its course.
Smudge was now Boss Cat
since the black dog died
chasing a car.

# Touch

On the road to Dublin
I listened to the click of Laurie's markers,
multi-coloured, shifting in her hands
as she arranged and rearranged them,
sensing each colour, watching for
a missing one.

In the beginning
it was Buddha beads,
sandalwood on a leather string.
She liked to touch them gently,
she liked the smell.
Then boot laces,
easy to run through her fingers .

On holidays in the Adirondaks
she discovered playing cards,
velvet to the touch,
always throwing away the Joker,
clearing the deck.

After a while she started to hum,
recalling her playlist,
then sang to herself before asking
"How far to Exit Eight Dad?"
and a stop at McDonald's!

# Night Watchman

Lately, I can't
drink after six
unless I want to spend
half the night
like a night watchman
pacing quietly
between bed
and the loo
and back without
disturbing the silence.

People have written novels
through sleepless nights,
 like one American author
 whose name I can't remember.
It will come to me.
Yes, William Faulkner,
*As I Lay Dying*.

I am healthy, can walk, talk coherently,
even run when my head is clear
and finish a five-kilometre race
in a good time for my age.

 Can I accept the one certainty
my life promises me?
To age and go in peace?
Am I growing wiser?
Am I ripening?
Am I growing deeper and fuller?
Am I growing into myself?

# Speak her name

A legend on a T-shirt invited me
to speak her name.
On the busy street, I said
"Gillian Mary Fitzpatrick",
proclaiming the name of the woman I love.
I remember when Laurie called out
our friend Adrienne's name
again and again
until we asked her to stop.
"No," said Adrienne." It helps me to hear my name.
I need to proclaim my love for myself,
silence my critic."
I spoke my own name,
"John Bennett Riordan",
on Grafton Street.
Physician, heal thyself.

# Wild Swimmers

At a cold concrete pier in Ballylickey
they gather, "Ladies who Swim",
a hardy bunch who enjoy the embrace of the sea.
In freezing February or mad March,
later in summer temperatures
they plunge in
for a mind, body, spirit boost,
conquering fear and living the moment,
laughing and sometimes screaming
as they hit the cold water
or when a seal's head pops up among them.
Not thinking about what's been or what's next,
they feel alive and grateful,
knowing that they will feel better
afterwards as their flesh glows
and their hearts rejoice
at a grand sense of achievement.
"If you can do this you can do anything,"
might be their motto.
All different, they share each other's lives
through their love of the sea
and afterwards at an occasional coffee,
support each other with life's ups and downs.

# Minds

Great minds think alike.
Or foolish ones?
Both.

# Night

Night's mackerel sky
covers the Milky Way.
No birds sing.

# Dusk

A hawk flies from the dark wood,
followed soon by another.
Could they be nesting so close?

# For Patricia

I lay my back  on the plinth,
stretched my arms back to hers.
She stood behind me,
cradling my head.
Tall, fair hair,
warm open smile
reflecting her
courageous spirit.
Fond friend.
In my head
wild horses bucked and whinnied.
I muttered awkward words of affection.
"You felt your own strength," she said.

# Cherchez la femme

A woman whose smile lights up the room,
fine in mind and body,
feisty and not to be trifled with,
a thinker, sharp and incisive,
contemplative gardener
drawing energy from the soil,
great friend and mother,
nurturing with love.
You enrich my life.

# Murder in Manor Kilbride

At Manor Kilbride, that magic place
where the Shankhill River
flows through woodland
into the Upper Liffey,
we stood bewildered
on our camping holiday,
studying the remains of a raven
and her nestlings
blown to pieces
by a sheepman
with both barrels of a shotgun,
to be sure, to be sure,
fearing a raven picking the eyes
from his lambs.
The nest lies in smithereens
around the dead birds.

Later at dusk we watched
bats flitting about over the stream
in the shadows.
In a fit of bravado I said,
"What's the bets I can't hit
a bat with my pellet gun?"
(an old Slavia that I smuggled into the house).
My pals laughed hysterically.
Goaded, I swept the darkness
and followed a bat, pulling the trigger
as the creature turned away

The bat fell on some stones,
a wing clipped by my pellet.

The boys were silent,
I was filled with remorse.
The story told many times afterwards.
A shot in a million,
no sitting duck.
I sold the Slavia the following Monday.

# Season's End

That morning it seemed like
a vandal had slashed the blue autumn sky
clouds leaking through the wounds.
I stopped to greet the widow seeking herself
in a sea of grief over her mate of thirty years,
drawing water from her well of loneliness.
Temperatures dropped
as the summer vacationers
headed home to work and school
after a vintage summer of swimming
in Mediterranean temperatures
on the Wild Atlantic Way,
their dreams of barbecues,
outdoor tennis matches
realised, their children fast asleep in the back of the car.

# Winter Quest

I saw a fox looking lost
in the field beside us,
one of the travelling dog foxes
on a long walk seeking a mate
outside his territory,
driven by his need to copulate.
Many don't make it
and are run over on unfamiliar roads.
Some ignore their regular garden feeding spots,
such is their quest for coition.
Others are called by the frightening shrieks
of vixens in the darkness of winter nights.
Travel well, my clever friend.

# Straight lines

It's early morning; rooks have
already occupied Christy's
neatly ploughed field.
I admire the ploughman's skill
and geometry as straight lines
fall along parallel furrows from
a flat turntable beside the road to
the cottage below. Cawing rooks
are joined by cackling jackdaws.
The brown landscape seethes with life
and sound as the ground is prepared for
another crop.

# Kelp

In winter, after a storm,
I collect kelp washed on the beach
to refresh the good earth
in a bed that yielded
a record crop of kale last year.
In spite of a battle with slugs
and the white butterfly caterpillar,
a voracious feeder,
fruits de mer  et la terre.

# Winter visitor

Hiking down the road to the sea,
I am surprised by a snipe bursting from
its wetland sanctuary, on a a zig zagging flight
across the field as if to avoid possible hunters.
In the breeding season snipe climb high in the sky
and in a steep dive create a bleating or drumming sound
    with their tail feathers
giving them in some parts the name"airy goats".
Others call our winter visitor's behaviour
    "winnowing."

# Otter Watch

Cycling on the Baltimore road from Skibb,
Before the "Great Disturbance",
The Ilen is full with tide.
At 7 am I stop for a rest at the New Bridge.
Suddenly an otter surfaces beside me and
in a fluid forward roll dives,
as surprised as I am.
Much later on the narrow road to Glandore,
a lost otter lopes along,
finding a way back to the sea.
I spot a family group
off the pier in Glandore.
Gifts bestowed by Mother Nature,
a state of grace to be savoured.

# Morning

As I walk down the sea road,
flanked by a steep hillside of luscious green grass
to the south and a wet boggy field to the north,
my head heavy and spirits low,
two wild duck rise from the marsh
and circle the valley, quacking,
followed by a third as they
gain sight of the sea.
No sheep grazing on the rich grass
 of the southern slope.
Dog trouble perhaps?
Cattle and two horses graze on the poor land
to the north.
The three mallard return, still circling the fields
like fighters preparing to fly off on a sortie.
No sign of the solitary snipe visiting from northern
    Europe.
My fog lifts as I turn for home.